Seeds Of Songs

Copyright © Michael J. Peade 2020

All rights reserved.

This book is copyright. Apart from any fair dealing for the purposes of private study, research, criticism or review as permitted under the copyright Act, no part may be reproduced, stored in a retrieval system, or transmitted, in any form by any means of electronic, mechanical, photocopying, recording or otherwise without prior written permission. Inquiries to be made to the author.

First published in 2020.

National Library of Australia,
Cataloguing-in-Publication entry:

Seeds Of Songs

ISBN 978-0-646-82551-9

Peade, Michael John, 1963 -

© Cover Photography by: Janelle Andrea Watson
Publisher: PeadeSongs

To my family
~

About the writer

Michael has been writing song lyrics for over 40 years.

He started by writing poetry at an early age, but soon realised he had a talent and passion, for putting words into musicians and performers mouths.

He began writing lyrics for songs when he was asked by a friend who was in a Sydney rock band. The band had plenty of great music, but no words to complete some of their songs. Michael wrote a lyric, which the band quickly took on, recorded, and began to perform live at their many gigs around Sydney, Australia.

He will never forget the day he heard his words come alive. 'It was a satisfying moment and the start of a writing journey.'

He went on to write more lyrics for the bands music before forming working relationships with other bands and musicians, both locally and nationally. He still writes poetry, but lyric writing remains his passion.

Since then, he has written and collaborated on many songs. His co-writers are now located internationally and include, Australia, the United Kingdom, New York, Los Angeles, Arizona, Texas, Spain, Russia, and Nashville.

He has a catalogue of over 700 song lyrics and has had over 160 of these songs demoed and recorded by various artists.

He also wrote the musical rock operas, "Adam and Eve – A Tale" and "The Pink Caravan". The original script and lyrics for the plays were composed by Michael, while the music was written by Harvey Welsh.

He is a member of the Australian Performing Rights Association, (APRA/AMCOS) and continues to write and provide lyrics to many musicians and bands internationally.

Preface
~

In the pages ahead are the works of words, poems, lyrics, and songs that have filled my life.

Some of these works are close to my heart; others are close to my bones. Some of them have come alive in song; others have been left dusty on the shelf of time.

Added between the song lyrics in this book are extracts from the many other works I have written that haven't made this edition.

The many years I have spent composing my words for musicians, stage plays, and other writers have brought me much joy, at times frustration, but ultimately a release for creativity, challenge, satisfaction, and, in the end, completeness.

I hope you enjoy my words; some are inspired by many great writers, bands, performers, life itself, and those close to me; others I do not even know. Some have personal meaning to me; some do not. Some may have resonated within me without any direct personal experience or thought. Some come from an idea or a subject to build creativity. To me, the meaning is always open to interpretation by the reader or listener to make their own connection and feeling to what the poem, lyric, or song are about.

Over time and with effort, mixed with that inner passion and belief in what we love to do, we can all reach the goals that we set out to achieve, and one of those goals and loves for me has always been writing and turning words into song.

For all of my family, friends, fellow co-writers, readers, and listeners, I thank you for your encouragement, belief, and support in helping me to make my words come to life, and for the ones that I have never had music written for, they just sit firmly on a page.

Music, like life, takes us on a journey.

The journey of music and words will always hold a place and time in our life!

Music for the creator is an expression, a feeling, a release, a work, a talent.

To the listener, it provides harmony, peace, love, sense, fun and enjoyment.

It is a gift to us all.

Michael J. Peade
December 2007

CONTENTS

~

About the writer	vi
Preface	vii

Stone In My Shoe	15
A Life Filled With Love	16
Yesterday's Sins	17
Every Moment I Get Closer	19
Bleeding	20
Emerald Bay	21
Careless Moment	23
Bridge To No-Where	24
Second Skin	25
In The Rain	27
Bend And Change	28
Is He Anything Like Me	29
I'm Not Gonna Give Up The Dream	31
Harmony	32
In The Morning	33
In Your Arms Again	35
Fall From Grace	36
Don't Be Too Afraid	37
Paint That Look	39
Where The River Used To Go	40
No Trouble At All	41
The Last Words	43
When You Know Who You Are	44
Try Not To Say Too Much	45
All About Love	47
I Don't Call This House My Home	48
Stranger In My Dreams	49

When It's All Over	51
All Of My Mistakes	52
Softly Spoken Words	53
Dreams Don't Make Reality	55
I See A Change	56
Back Then	57
Broken And Busted	59
Sometimes	60
It's True	61
Catch Me	63
Now Or Never	64
Why	65
Lost Together	67
In A Minute	68
Scream Louder	69
Hope In Us All	71
Emotion	72
Perpetual Devotion	73
Cold Silence	75
Desperation	76
Crystal Glass	77
Bourbon Street	79
Pretending You Know My Name	80
Preying For Love	81
Crime City	83
Our Own Eyes	84
Elaine	85
Blues In My Veins	87
Don't Let It Go Tonight	88
Love Ends With A Whisper	89
Don't Go Losing Hope	91
While The City Sleeps	92
Salvation	93
Where I Wanna Be	95

Would You	96
All Aboard	97
My Hurt	99
Out Of My Depth	100
What's Going On	101
That's Just What Happens	103
Ignite	104
Time To Be Me	105
Hurt Me Breaking The Rules	107
You Defy Me	108
Words I've Never Spoken	109
Fight On The Outside	111
The Future's Changing The Past	112
Hurricane	113
Make Believe	115
Ballad Of Surprise	116
Tell Me	117
Feeling Lonely	119
Family	120
Heart On My Sleeve	121
My Day Has Come	123
All That Remains	124
My Breath	125
Burnt Out	126
Reasons	128
Together We Can Shine	129
At First Light	130
You're Here Now	131
Some Reason Now	132
Stranded Heart	134
Yesterday's News	135
Remember	136
Stir Crazy	137
Enough About Love	138

Reflections Of A Bad Day	140
Not Going Down Like The Sun	141
Piece Of Mind	142
Frost	144
Politics	145
All I Can Hope For	146
The Sun Has No Light	147
Releases	148
Acknowledgements	150

STONE IN MY SHOE

Felt the bite last night from the coldness
My voice was stale from the rain
My face has the wrinkles and the coldness
Hides what my heart calls pain

Every step I take has new direction
North, south, east and west we ride
Through the mountains to the rivers in the valley
Sometimes a man has no place to hide

Another door closes in my way
Another night we sing the blues
Another day passes on the calendar
I've got another stone in my shoe
I've got another stone in my shoe

Break the ice that is below my feet
Let me see the cold light of day
The things I heard you say I believed
Now I wish that I had made the break

Far away I see the mountains
Where the winters rage will hide my fears
Those parks where they have those fountains
Don't hide the ghosts that are near

Another door closes in my way
Another night we sing the blues
Another day passes on the calendar
I've got another stone in my shoe

Another night seems to slowly fade
Cause in and out of love we move
Another night we sleep then we wake
I've got another stone in my shoe
I've got another stone in my shoe

A Life Filled With Love

I used to have this feeling
A paradise in the rough
Rusty chains all around me
Faded images in the dust
Everything seemed so hard to hold
The early days were without soul
Now you've given me this spirit
That warms me when I'm cold

Now you've given me the strength to carry on
Something special to hold on to
I see it all different now
Deep down I see the proof

There's a feeling in my heart
That keeps me shining through
Pressures eased inside of me
I've come out of this make believe
I've got a life, a life filled with love

I know it took a little time
I wanted the impossible dream
Growing up through the shadows
Tracing the places that I've been
Now this gold and silver linen
Rises when I'm kissing you
Muddy waters disappear
As soon as we make the move

There's a feeling in my heart
That keeps me shining through
Pressures eased inside of me
I've come out of this make believe
I've got a life, a life filled with love
There's a feeling in my heart
That keeps me shining through
Pressures eased inside of me
I've come out of this make believe
I've got a life, a life filled with love

Yesterday's Sins

I see the flame burning
Can't help thinking about tomorrow
Watching the road in front of me
I see the cars turn against the arrows

And the light travels
To a distant fence
And the glory we found
Found its way into different hands

Before we had it all
But we lost the games we couldn't win
It's an endless fight that lasts forever
Our dreams are yesterday's sins
Our dreams are yesterday's sins

We played songs
That helped us through the shadows
We strayed from richness
That kept us feeling we had it

But this light held
No true defense
And the glory we found
Found its way into different hands

Before we had it all
But we lost the games we couldn't win
It's an endless fight that lasts forever
Our dreams are yesterday's sins

Our dreams are yesterday's sins

"I can't see the sun shining, as bright as it used to be. I can't see the flowers growing in between the trees. I can't see through the darkness, so what's the hope of finding, the secrets that I lost one day, waiting for the sun to start shining"

Sometimes the lyric comes easy, sometimes it takes a little while for something tangible.

EVERY MOMENT I GET CLOSER

Let me breathe again
Like a page with written words
Beneath the silhouette of night
Silence is the only sound I heard
Let me find the key
To forget these troubled times
You letting me be me
Means more to me than life

Let me watch the rain
Fall on the colours that make the night
Let me fly away
Beyond the morning light

And let the candle burn
To light the darkest night
Cause every moment I get closer
My dreams are taking flight
And let my body learn
The gentle touch of your caress
Cause every moment I get closer
To your love and tenderness

Let me live again
Mend a broken heart with mine
Beneath the skin you're bleeding
And retreating all the time
Let me watch the rain
Fall on the colours that make the night
Let me fly away
Beyond the morning light

And let the candle burn
To light the darkest night
Cause every moment I get closer
My dreams are taking flight
And let my body learn
The gentle touch of your caress
Cause every moment I get closer
To your love and tenderness

BLEEDING

A careless heart is like a promise
So easy to break, no boundaries on it
When the minutes seem to turn to hours
Then we feel we've lost what we thought was ours

Then the bleeding starts
It never ends
It's on our fingers
It's on our hands
Through falling dreams
Through falling skies
They never see us
Through our own eyes
While we're bleeding
While we're bleeding

In the distance we see the debris
While our hearts linger with the smell of maybe
The wounds all heal, the scars all fade
They're so easy to create

Then the bleeding starts
It never ends
It's on our fingers
It's on our hands
Through falling dreams
Through falling skies
They never see us
Through our own eyes
While we're bleeding
While we're bleeding

Emerald Bay

Looking out over Emerald Bay
The shore seems so far away
On this hill I'd sit and wait
For some illusion to gently fade

I must have sat here a thousand times
I must have made this wish before
I must have shouted to someone out there
Cause I've never been this sure

And don't mind me I'm just the same
The same man I used to be
Cause this is where my secrets lie
Hidden somewhere between the waves
On some empty soul boat
I've been doing time on Emerald Bay

I made some wish here
Seems a thousand years ago
I put them in a bottle
I threw them into Emerald Bay

There was a time when I had my hands
Firmly on the wheel
Now the kids have all grown up
We've got some stories to tell

And don't mind me I'm just the same
The same man I used to be
Cause this is where my secrets lie
Hidden somewhere between the waves
On some empty soul boat
I've been doing time on Emerald Bay

I've been doing time, on Emerald Bay
I've been doing time, on Emerald Bay

"Sure there's an answer, to keep this world intact, fighting and believing, we have to face the facts. Sure there's an answer, we can treat them one by one, and we can keep this world from falling into the fire of the sun"

Careless Moment

I've seen a lifetime of promises, delivered in front of my eyes
I've been given a thousand reasons why
There is lightning in the skies
I've been given a thousand questions
Delivered in the palm of my hands
But never as hard as the ones, I'm now trying to understand

There goes another careless moment
Sliding through my fingers
Another wasted search, on a heart that lingers
Bound by a sword, held together with trust
Another careless moment, is turning brown with rust

I've weathered more than four seasons
Delivered tears from my eyes
The moss is slowly gathering around me
I hide behind all the lies
I've tried to soak up the anger, delivered from my lonely heart
Waiting for the second, that I can get past the past

There goes another careless moment
Sliding through my fingers
Another wasted search, on a heart that lingers
Bound by a sword, held together with trust
Another careless moment, is turning brown with rust

I've tried to soak up the anger
Delivered from my lonely heart
Waiting for the second
That I can get past the past

There goes another careless moment
Sliding through my fingers
Another wasted search, on a heart that lingers
Bound by a sword, held together with trust
Another careless moment, is turning brown with rust

Bridge To No-Where

There's a bridge to no-where at the end of my street
Where the children are playing, they're doing a hip beat
There's a bridge to no-where, man laid the first stone
Every morning we leave for work, at night we return home

There's a road with no lanes, no trees by its side
There's a shop and it's closed, the shopkeeper he died
And a blind man can see, see what's going on around here
There's a bridge to no-where, and that is what I fear

And it's taking us somewhere and I don't want to go
There's a bridge to no-where and there's no-where to row
The waters stopped running and god only knows
There's a bridge to no-where, where the howling wind blows
Our wires are crossed and it's cold, so cold

The flowers are dying, all the petals they dropped
The green and the red ones, they all lay where they have stopped
And the howling wind blows, blows up every night around here
There's an old lady who knows, she's seen it all before this year

And it's taking us somewhere and I don't want to go
There's a bridge to no-where and there's no-where to row
The waters stopped running and god only knows
There's a bridge to no-where, where the howling wind blows
Our wires are crossed and it's cold, so cold

There's a bridge to no-where at the end of my street
And I don't want my kids to all know
We've all got nails in our feet
There's a bridge to no-where and it's got us all beat
We just want to know all the secrets that it keeps
Our wires are crossed and it's cold, so cold

SECOND SKIN

I brace myself for a smooth second ride
Some things I can't get used to
Cut another moment to put aside
I still dream when I'm close to you

You say that you'd love to fly
Like a diamond through the sky
A warm faded moment always rings true
Your soft heart and warm ways
I fall flat if there's ever a day
I have to spend without you

I'd be your second skin
I'd move mountains to get in
I'd be your strength; I'd be your tide
I'd change a thousand sins
I'd be your second skin
I would be your blood supply

And I never stop needing you
And I never stop breathing you
And I never stop loving you
And I never stop wanting you

I'd be your second skin
I'd move mountains to get in
I'd be your strength; I'd be your tide
I'd change a thousand sins
I'd be your second skin
I would be your blood supply

You're a sweet moment in time
A sweet moment in life
You're a sweet moment and mine
And I'll never stop wanting you
I'd be your second skin

Recording in the studio with Richard Johnstone.

"Cause I'll be there waiting for you, I'll be the strong one, when you need someone to hold on too. Cause I'll be there, to catch your tears one by one, I'll be there with my shoulder to cry on"

Listening to the finished song with Richard.

In the Rain

Did you hear the church bells ringing
Ringing out across the ground
Across the mountains the streams been running
Carrying hope to a different town

Did you hear the angels calling
Their sweet whispers in the rain
Did you feel the gentle drops running
Through the streets to the sugar cane

And in the rain, comes another day
Washing away those tears of pain
And in the rain, angers left wet to dry
And the sun hides in the distant sky
In the rain, sweet smells save another day

Across the meadows the wheat's been dying
All the farmers they lost their way
Searching for some star that's falling
Or some dream that will come their way

Hands of time are slowly turning
Endless hours they make us late
Outside a fire's been burning
Down the road we've shut the gate

And in the rain, comes another day
Washing away those tears of pain
And in the rain, angers left wet to dry
And the sun hides in the distant sky
In the rain, sweet smells save another day

In the rain, the sweet smells save another day

BEND AND CHANGE

I've never played the game
Never broke any of the rules
I know what you're saying
There's still so much I have to prove

Feels like the morning
Is all empty and behind me
I share the same dreams
The same dreams you always told me

And just when you said I could go my own way
You bend and change, everything you had to say
I don't know why, it doesn't feel the same
I'm always dragging, another step behind

I've never had reason
Why I should be stopping you
I tried to understand
You were everything I had to lose

Feels like I'm breaking
It's all cut and dried
Never knowing that you
That you could change your mind

And just when you said I could go my own way
You bend and change, everything you had to say
I don't know why, it doesn't feel the same
I'm always dragging, another step behind

And just when I'm getting away
Running, falling through the mistakes
You hold me, you change me
My defenses start to break.

And just when you said I could go my own way
You bend and change, everything you had to say
I don't know why, it doesn't feel the same
I'm always dragging, another step behind

Is He Anything Like Me

When you look into the mirror
What do you really see
Is it a restless figure
A reflection of a memory
When you walked out the door
Does the sun set the same as before
Under the busy moonlight
Does he hold you, give you something more

Is he anything like me
Guess what got washed up from the sea
A small piece of wisdom, and a sweeping memory
On the sand there is a kiss, I wonder if you're really free
And if you do the same things, is he anything like me

Take away the blinding dust
Look at the world I delivered you
I took your hand and heart
We looked down from the highest view
Now every sunrise that shines
Proves a different light
And everything that was yours and mine
Has fallen out of sight

Is he anything like me
Guess what got washed up from the sea
A small piece of wisdom and a sweeping memory
On the sand there is a kiss, I wonder if you're really free
And if you do the same things, is he anything like me

Does he touch you like I did, does a soft kiss make you fall
Does it take much to lift the lid, have you ever been as sure

Is he anything like me
Guess what got washed up from the sea
A small piece of wisdom, and a sweeping memory
On the sand there is a kiss, I wonder if you're really free
And if you do the same things
Is he anything like me

"I'm numb, bring me some rain, wash away this eclipse of cloud, and bring me some freshness, clean skin and no doubt"

I'm Not Gonna Give Up The Dream

Searching through these visions I have
Looking for the direction I need
You were the one with my hand
But I let you slip through with ease

I had you in sight
But in the darkness you fade
I still remember the nights
And what it took to make me feel this way

I was chasing satisfaction
You were the one that I believed
I'm not gonna give up
I'm not gonna give up the dream

I try to keep control
To my feelings inside
Taking a grip and a hold
Shivering with fright

You always showed me
What I thought were the rules
But I see you break them
Like so many fools

Wondering lost in emotion
Wondering free
I'm not gonna give up
I'm not gonna give up the dream

These seconds are hours
These days turn to weeks
I was chasing satisfaction
You were the one I believed

I was chasing satisfaction
You were the one I believed
I'm not gonna give up
I'm not gonna give up the dream

HARMONY

I was standing where your shadow was
Now somehow I see
I'm falling down from above
You're the angel coming for me

Thought I could survive
Wipe my tears up on my sleeve
But now I know what I feel
Are dreams that I have to believe

Now all of my time is for you
Every breath I take, it cleans me
Now it's so easy to forget the mistakes
When we were living in harmony
When we were living in harmony

Sure I was new at love
I just hoped I could learn
When the mist falls down from above
Then I hope this road never turns

Now all of my time is for you
Every breath I take, it cleans me
Now it's so easy to forget the mistakes
When we were living in harmony
When we were living in harmony

Now all of my time is for you
Every breath I take, it cleans me
Now it's so easy to forget the mistakes
When we were living in harmony
When we were living in harmony

In The Morning

Goodnight kisses are felt, in a shaded room
Where no-one ever listens, to our rhythm and tune
Fortune don't come easy, but it's the dream of knowing
When the sun comes up, I'll see you in the morning

When the night passes through
While you are gently sleeping
I'll pull the satin covers over you
Before the sun rises in the morning
Reflecting in the dawn light
When love is gently waking
I'll hold onto last night, I'll see you in the morning

When the curtains close, and the day is almost done
Just inside our warming hearts, we'll hold tight to all our love
Cause outside the windows, it might be cold and raining
But inside our souls we know, this feeling will always start
Once again in the morning

When the night passes through
While you are gently sleeping
I'll pull the satin covers over you
Before the sun rises in the morning
Reflecting in the dawn light
When love is gently waking
I'll hold onto last night, I'll see you in the morning

And let all our troubles go
Let the moonlight gently pass them away
Cause just like yesterday in the morning
Together we'll start another day
When the night passes through
While you are gently sleeping
I'll pull the satin covers over you
Before the sun rises in the morning
Reflecting in the dawn light
When love is gently waking
I'll hold onto last night, I'll see you in the morning

"You're afraid to be in my arms, let go, let love shine, because it may last for an eternity"

In Your Arms Again

Deep inside there is a space, with a soul full of tenderness
Deep within there is a collision
Of some warm and cold emptiness
But everyday grows a feeling of closeness
And all I know, there is no harm
Because the soft ache turns to healing I guess
In a matter of time I'll be in your arms

Cause every day you are gone, I walk on shells as brittle as bone
Seeing every moment go bye, feels like a million years alone

In your arms again, tight full of warmth is all the proof
Another feeling of soaring high
Above the clouds on the worlds roof
Wishing that it never ends
Every moment becomes so smooth
When I am in your arms again
Holding another moment we can't lose

A soft breeze whispers in my ear
A voice I know too good and well
Keeps me pure and at ease
Through the times I could have fell
Cause every day comes a corner
Another bend to your door
Another soft kiss gently waits
We both won't have to wait anymore

And every day, grows a feeling of closeness
And all I know, there is no harm
Because the soft ache turns to healing I guess
In a matter of time I'll be in your arms

In your arms again, tight full of warmth is all the proof
Another feeling of soaring high
Above the clouds on the worlds roof
Wishing that it never ends
Every moment becomes so smooth
When I am in your arms again
Holding another moment we can never lose

Fall From Grace

I can't control this feeling inside
That takes me high like a bird
It holds me like a feathered cloud
And leaves me without any words

I can't deny this open hand
Reaches for lost emptiness
If I died tomorrow would you understand
My level of faithfulness

And all your promises, they left a bad stain
The hurt only stopped us, and you can't build it again

When we fall from grace, from our old wooden chairs
When all we do is go chasing, what we thought was better left
Spending time running, hearts find another place
Something must be missing, when we fall from grace
Something must be missing, when we fall from grace

Now where is the heartbreak
Left hidden in empty rooms
Moving from feeling to feeling
We forget what we had so soon

Now all these frozen times, keep a line of bitter sight
And all we seem to find, is the same empty night

When we fall from grace, from our old wooden chairs
When all we do is go chasing, what we thought was better left
Spending time running, hearts find another place
Something must be missing, when we fall from grace
Something must be missing, when we fall from grace

Don't Be Too Afraid

I don't want to have to tell you
Hiding from you behind this mask
But pressure tends to get the best of me
When you do too much too fast

I remember from the first time
When you took my arm and shook my hand
With that skin so soft
You'd never have to say too much
To make me understand

So don't be too afraid
To say what's really on your mind
You know you'll have me doubling back
With every single line
Just take me on the long run
Take me all the way through the gates
Take some time off and surround this man
Just don't be too afraid

You say to me these are headlines
These games are what people like to read
You can see these scripts at the movies
Police hear them from the thieves

And I remember from the first time
When you took my arm and shook my hand
With that skin so soft
You'd never have to say too much
To make me understand

So don't be too afraid
To say what's really on your mind
You know you'll have me doubling back
With every single line
Just take me on the long run
Take me all the way through the gates
Take some time off and surround this man
Just don't be too afraid
Don't be too afraid

"I'll just dream on, I can wait for time, until my arms are locked, and locked for life. And I will save the memories one by one, until another day, I'll just dream on"

Paint That Look

Hold that look still, the one in the light
Against those red roses, you're shining tonight
Don't be mistaken, or disguise that smooth face
Your eyes are like diamonds, I can't keep myself straight

Can I paint that look, colour it for a start
There's a jewel in your soul, there's gold in your heart
Can I paint that look, trust my hands I trust you
It's a miracle you hold me, can I paint that look
So I have the proof

I can't fall any further; your charm fills this room
The flame burns warmer; we get closer with every move
Don't you be needing, the last breath that I take
Your eyes are like diamonds, I can't keep myself straight

Can I paint that look, colour it for a start
There's a jewel in your soul, there's gold in your heart
Can I paint that look, trust my hands I trust you
It's a miracle you hold me, can I paint that look
So I have the proof

Can I paint that look, colour it for a start
There's a jewel in your soul, there's gold in your heart
Can I paint that look, trust my hands I trust you
It's a miracle you hold me, can I paint that look
So I have the proof

If you need it, the last breath that I take
I'll hold it for you, I can't keep myself straight

WHERE THE RIVER USED TO GO

Dark nights could never explain
The things we used to see around here
Through the mountains and in between
A river used to run through here

There was a place further down
Where an old house used to be
People came from all around
To hear the river speak

And not for one moment
Did you hear a whisper say
That these waters edges
Would run dry through this place

That's where the river used to go
That's where the river used to wind
Through the mountains and in between
That's where love used to hide

Down there time stood still
There was a land made of gold
Some had their soul saved
Their fortunes were forever told

And not for one moment
Did you hear a whisper say
That these waters edges
Would run dry through this place

That's where the river used to go
That's where the river used to wind
Through the mountains and in between
That's where love used to hide

That's where the river used to go
That's where dreams were easy to find
Through the mountains and in between
That's where love used to hide

No Trouble At All

When the truth unfolds
And the lies are put away
When the hurt is buried
And the search begins for a new day

You can call me
I'll listen content
To your sweet voice I manage
To bring my soul to land

Cause it will be no trouble
Just a minor stand
To reach out and touch you
To tell you the plan
About a dream forever
To touch your soul
A guiding light from heaven
It's the truth, it's no trouble at all
It's no trouble, no trouble at all

Don't be afraid to listen
Even if your ears burn
There's hope in holding
Words that make you learn

Shake the ghost that haunts you
Picture yourself in glory
I'll be there next to you
When you tell the story

Cause it will be no trouble
Just a minor stand
To reach out and touch you
To tell you the plan
About a dream forever
To touch your soul
A guiding light from heaven
It's the truth, it's no trouble at all
It's no trouble, no trouble at all

"Falling has never been so hard, hitting the ground I'm dusted off. With a head full of smarts, composure and a laugh, I pick up the change I lost"

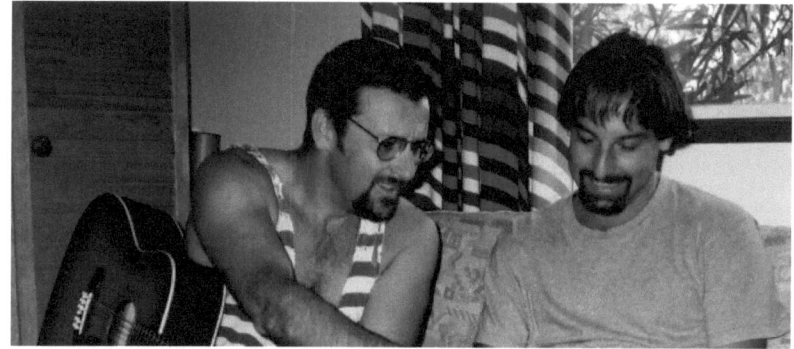
Conjuring up new music and the lyrics with Richard.

THE LAST WORDS

The last words ring through my mind
The last words like the last time
Seem to last forever in my heart
Forever in my heart I feel the pain
Those endless words I can't complain
About the things I used to feel
The last words keep those feelings deep inside

And though it ends and time goes on
I've got to try, cause the last words
Not the last thing on my mind
And though it seems a lonely world
I've begun to find
The last words, not the last thing on my mind

And only when I lost your hand
Did I feel the pain you must have felt
And only when I looked around
Did I feel the promises I should have kept
Those endless words I can't complain
About the things I used to feel
The last words keep those feelings deep inside

And though it ends and time goes on
I've got to try, cause the last words
Not the last thing on my mind
And though it seems a lonely world
I've begun to find
The last words, not the last thing on my mind

And though it seems an endless road
There's no place to hide to come back down
And as the door is slowly closed
I look for a voice that pulled me out

And though it ends and time goes on
I've got to try, cause the last words
Not the last thing on my mind

WHEN YOU KNOW WHO YOU ARE

Feel a soft breeze, a winter's air
Climbing high and far
Like love through broken years
Mending broken hearts
Feel a soft hand, another second
That brings a gift of light
Shining down on you
Bringing hope to a lonely night

They're just some things
They're just some ways
That led you near and far
Mending broken bridges
You know everything
When you know who you are

Feel the soft breeze, on your face
And when it feels it's leaving a mark
Pull away, dry the tears
Stand tall and leave the past

They're just some things
They're just some ways
That led you near and far
Mending broken bridges
You know everything
When you know who you are

And when you find yourself
A soft voice a soft hand
Remember where you came from
Where you were, now where you are

They're just some things
They're just some ways
That led you near and far
Mending broken bridges
You know everything
When you know who you are

TRY NOT TO SAY TOO MUCH

My foot is always in my mouth
I'm always trying to find an easy way out
From the traps I get myself in
Seems my words are my only sins

I feel I'm losing you with the truth
Out in the cold is nothing new to me
Win or lose it's all just the same
I'm just trying to tell you honestly

I'll try not to say too much
Then I think you'll find a better man
I'll cut back on some of the words
Then maybe you will understand

Falling short I'm an ocean away
Tell me if I'm just wasting my time
The bleeding could be stopped any day
If better words were easier to find

I know I'm trying hard at romance
I just gotta try and make some sense
Action speaks louder than words
I'll try and make a difference

I'll try not to say too much
Then I think you'll find a better man
I'll cut back on some of the words
Then maybe you will understand

I'll try not to say too much
I'll be a fool of a lesser kind
I'll give it to you all in touch
Keep my words to myself in my mind

I'll try not to say too much
Some of the things I say could turn you away
I'll try not to say too much
Before the dreams I have go drifting away

"And all those tears we cried, flowed to the end, a lonely heartbeat inside, ended when. All those tears dried, and we walked away, on a love we built, on better days"

All About Love

It's falling off my clothes
Like a wasted sun in the rain
Hiding light stained auras
It always shows, it always remains

The breeze feels like plum
And I don't ask why
Cause I know all the answers
In my mind it's a matter of time

I'll guide you, I'll show you
All about love, all about love
Like a wet tear running
Never seems quite enough
When it's all about love
Never seems quite enough

I feel like a rock
When my heart is so stained
I'm leaving for places
In this magical secret game

It's suddenly all clear
In your eyes it is all written
Hiding behind all these fears
Getting closer to what we're missing

I'll guide you, I'll show you
All about love, all about love
Like a wet tear running
Never seems quite enough
When it's all about love
Never seems quite enough

Sometimes I can't speak
Suddenly I'm lost for words
Cause falling at your feet, just might hurt
When it's all about love
Never seems quite enough

I Don't Call This House My Home

I've got nothing left to give
I've to put this jigsaw back together
I've lost every reason to live
I never thought you'd leave me forever

I've got to build this house again
I've got to put back on the phone
You still call me a friend
But while you're gone
I don't call this house my home

While you're gone
I don't call this house my home

I've watched everything flow down the stream
Watched it all flow out to sea
What did all those questions mean
I didn't think you'd easily forget about me

And just like all this rain
That comes and goes in this storm
You still call me a friend
But while you're gone
I don't call this house my home

While you're gone
I don't call this house my home

It might take a while
I've got to put back on the phone
I'll change the curtains and the blinds
But while you're gone
I don't call this house my home

While you're gone
I don't call this house my home

STRANGER IN MY DREAMS

I close my eyes to sleep
To curve the emotion that sweeps me
I can't explain these pictures
That take over me tonight, every night

Someday I'm going to wake up, so high but in deep
I'm going to look her up, and see who she really is

And I find you
When I close my eyes
I hold you
And feel you close to me
I want to go back
To where I've just been
Holding the stranger
The stranger in my dreams

I turn in my sleep, restless from these illusions I see
My life's so incomplete, not knowing my destiny

And I hold on tight
In the middle of the night
That's when I lose control
It cuts me like a knife
In the middle of the night
When I lose her hold

And I find you
When I close my eyes
I hold you
And feel you close to me
I want to go back
To where I've just been
Holding the stranger
The stranger in my dreams
I want to go back
To where I've just been
Holding the stranger
The stranger in my dreams

"Someone must be there, to hear the words about my children, tell me what I'm feeling, believe me what I say, I hope they never see this empty morning, this empty morning too close away"

Inspiration comes anytime.

WHEN IT'S ALL OVER

I don't know how I've come this far
To see it all escape, to see it all fall down
I've tried so hard, but all in vain
To keep my life, going the same way

When it's all over
It begins to change
Then you see mistakes
You didn't mean to make
When it's all over
When it's all over

The road we found, seems crazy now
Without demands, you never count
We never wished the same, through the days
Our whispers fade, in different ways

When it's all over
It begins to change
Then you see mistakes
You didn't mean to make
When it's all over
When it's all over

Now that we've made the break, I have to say
It's harder now, then it's ever been
I never thought, I could miss this life
Changing now, in front of me

When it's all over
You begin to break
You see the words
You didn't mean to make

When it's all over
It begins to change
Then you see mistakes
You didn't mean to make
When it's all over
When it's all over

All Of My Mistakes

I'm not proud, I've lost so much this time
I've cried out loud, tried to reach what I couldn't find
I know now, I can't change what I break
I can't turn around, all of my mistakes

I've been there too many times
I've had it in my hands
It seemed too high to climb
I've felt the rain fall like feathers and weights
They both leave a stain
All of my mistakes

I've looked forward, there's a certainty inside of me
If I believe it all, I can set myself a new dream
An open mind this time, will keep my world at bay
Give me time to heal, all of my mistakes

I've been there too many times
I've had it in my hands
It seemed too high to climb
I've felt the rain fall like feathers and weights
They both leave a stain
All of my mistakes

It just might take a moment, it just might take a while
If I can throw it all away, over a million miles

I've been there too many times
I've had it in my hands
It seemed too high to climb
I've felt the rain fall like feathers and weights
They both leave a stain
All of my mistakes

Softly Spoken Words

It's so hard to show you, all the things I've been feeling
All the things I felt left me cold and needing
And my heart was closed, to everything I knew
My heart knows something, we all get too choose

Some kind of trust, some kind of love
Some kind of feeling, somewhere got lost

We all get to speak words of wisdom
We all get to speak words of rhyme
Without you I cannot give you
Every second, every moment of my life

Softly speaking I can't show you
What you mean to me this time
I can only whisper softly
The words that mean all time

You said you knew me, your face shining in the night
I was trying to remind you, that everything is all right
I've always told you, everything from deep inside
But my heart knows something, it didn't need to fight

Some kind of trust, some kind of love
Some kind of feeling, somewhere got lost

We all get to speak words of wisdom
We all get to speak words of rhyme
Without you I cannot give you
Every second, every moment of my life

Softly speaking I can't show you
What you mean to me this time
I can only whisper softly
The words that mean all time

"Every dog has its day, every man finds a way to stop falling into the deep end"

Dreams Don't Make Reality

Here I go another morning again
Another heart I just can't tame
There you go falling, weak through my hands
Are you ever going to stop this rain

And I watch you smile, and you light this room
I'm falling flat, trying to get to you

I tried to make you see
You're staring right through me
In the darkest light, you fall, you fade
I crash so hard, I start, I break
Believing dreams don't make, dreams don't make reality

You leave without a whisper
You move without a sound
Falling through weathered fingers
You're pulling any good moment down

I watch the time piece, slowly ticking away
Made the same mistake, I'm going to have to change

I tried to make you see
You're staring right through me,
In the darkest light, you fall, you fade
I crash so hard, I start, I break
Believing dreams don't make, dreams don't make reality

Every dream I build, seems to fall back down
Like an empty moment I'm left in time
And every word I spoke, tried to bring you around
But I can't reach, I can't change your mind

I tried to make you see
You're staring right through me
In the darkest light, you fall, you fade
I crash so hard, I start, I break
Believing dreams don't make
Dreams don't make reality

I SEE A CHANGE

I see over the rippled water
Reflections from the sky
A lonely star looking back at me
Trying to find the answers why

I fell over some rough terrain
And I stumbled along for a ride
Hoping that I'd find your heart
Ready to let me inside

You don't know what's around the corner
But I see a window of opportunity
I don't know how I'd begin to speak
If you were closer to me

And I know that it's only time until you tell
That every lonely man
Has been to heaven, he's been to hell
Seems a likely story, but today must be your day
Cause right now I'm confessing
I see a change

I'm turning round this lonely bend
Heading for a hilltop coated green
Passed another lonely track
Where the jagged edges line the streets

You don't know what's around the corner
But I see a window of opportunity
I don't know how I'd begin to speak
If you were closer to me

And I know that it's only, time until you tell
That every lonely man
Has been to heaven, he's been to hell
Seems a likely story, but today must be your day
Cause right now I'm confessing
I see a change
I see a change

BACK THEN

I'm sitting by this creek, in this castle camp
Years ago I left a bad feeling, different kind of life back then

Seems only yesterday, when I packed all my bags
When life back then, was one big seasoned drag

Now every night I light a lamp
And it shines for days
I won't let anything get in my way
And I won't be tempted then
Like it was only yesterday
When I remember when

I went to work, and I bled for a crust
When I went to work, in a city without trust
And I tackled everything, like no tomorrow
And my only sin, was returning what I burrowed
Back then, when I remember when

Long ago was a little wild, every day the same old way
Trying hard to hold a smile, every night I'd sit and pray

It all seemed sour, now life's so very sweet
When I look back then, it was a lonely one-way street

Now every night I light a lamp
And it shines for days
I won't let anything get in my way
And I won't be tempted then
Like it was only yesterday
When I remember when

Like it was only yesterday
I won't be tempted again
Like it was only yesterday
When I remember when

"The black night makes me afraid, I live beneath my bed, the foundations have been laid, I'm a man-made nervous wreck"

BROKEN AND BUSTED

Been down a lonely highway
Dealt cards I've never seen
Tried to do it all the right way
Changed mistakes I didn't mean

This sun beats a warm wave
Turning dark nights into day
But it's still your soft kiss
That I can never turn away

I've had a cold hand that pulled some fate
I've had a cold heart, just hope it's not too late

Been broken and busted, been down but I'm not out
Been broken and busted, seen dreams die in a drought
Sometimes there's no way knowing
When your world is inside out
I've been broken and busted
Mend me pull me out

A winter's night is cold
A sinking feeling slips through
Summer days burn a hole
I never meant to hurt you

Some things can cut
Just like words is a sword
Down sun-drenched highways
Come help push me forward

I've had a cold hand that pulled some fate
I've had a cold heart, just hope it's not too late

Been broken and busted, been down but I'm not out
Been broken and busted, seen dreams die in a drought
Sometimes there's no way knowing
When your world is inside out
I've been broken and busted
Mend me pull me out

SOMETIMES

Sometimes I think of memories
That just won't go away
Sometimes I think of some dream
I had some other day
Sometimes I wonder why
I got lost along this road
Sometimes I think of surrendering
From carrying this heavy load

And sometimes I just behave
The way I used to as a boy
But just keep reminding me
Stop the tears and enjoy

I can't grasp this feeling
I can't tell you why
I'd have to be holding the answers
Sometimes the truth is blind
I just want the memories
The ones that are better kept
For the grace of always knowing
Sometimes yesterday is better left

Sometimes I hold within me
A feeling that only burns
Sometimes I can't escape
The feelings just return
Sometimes beneath the surface
I scratch the skin I make it bleed
Sometimes a sleeping memory
Is all the proof I need

I can't grasp this feeling
I can't tell you why
I'd have to be holding the answers
Sometimes the truth is blind
I just want the memories
The ones that are better kept
For the grace of always knowing
Sometimes yesterday is better left

It's True

I've seen you walk out the door, so many times before
You keep coming back when it's said and done
I've seen you crying, but you always seem to call
I don't know if you're winning in the long run

It's just a restless ride I'm going through
I know there's got to be some compromise

Cause your telling me
Telling me it's true
No matter what time of day
All the things you have to say
Are just the proof
You're telling me it's true

I've seen you hold out your hand, a thousand times before
You're pushing me when I'm against the wind
I know it might not matter, but I know you're in my heart
My world without you feels so cold

It's just a restless ride I'm going through
I know there's got to be some compromise

Cause your telling me
Telling me to choose
No matter what time of day
All the things you have to say
Are just the proof
You're telling me it's true

Don't you know, don't you know, I'm needing you
I want to give, I want to give, something back to you

Cause your telling me
Telling me it's true
No matter what time of day
All the things you have to say
Are just the proof
You're telling me it's true

"Trust dies slowly, a helping hand is rusting fast, and I don't want to die knowing, time fell through an hourglass"

With the great Harvey Welsh, co-writer and musical genius.

In the studio with Harvey, working on new material.

CATCH ME

There are things
That don't make any sense
Times when you sit
On that big fence

Doesn't matter what you know
It comes together some how

Catch me when I'm falling
Save me where you stand
Catch me when I'm flying
Throw me your hands

Just when you frown
You grab me, force me down
You play a game
That sits so strange

Doesn't matter what you know
It comes together some how

Catch me when I'm falling
Save me where you stand
Catch me when I'm flying
Throw me your hands

Doesn't matter what you know
It comes together some how

Catch me when I'm falling
Save me where you stand
Catch me when I'm flying
Throw me your hands

NOW OR NEVER

I moved slowly
Through the numbness of the same
And I washed of the memory
That I'd caught in the rain
Maybe I should have known
But I was angry and I'd like to wait
For the curtain to open
Before bitter love on your face

You said it was too cold, you said it was too late

Then you stood in the doorway
With your shadow growing louder
Your lips started to move
And I heard you speak
It was all too faded
And my ears couldn't believe what I was hearing
You said it was now or never
Now or never

I needed you now
More than the reality of haste
I'd built on some moment
That had left an empty space
I should have seen the signs
That the road we had taken
Was wet and slippery
With pieces that were broken

You said it was too cold, you said it was too late

Then you stood in the doorway
With your shadow growing louder
Your lips started to move
And I heard you speak
It was all too faded
And my ears couldn't believe what I was hearing
You said it was now or never
Now or never

WHY

There's a bitter taste
Left in my mouth
A winding road I've followed
A twisted life
Of borrowed time
And I don't know
Why I bothered

Maybe it's just an empty dream
Maybe it's just me

I don't know why
I don't know why
I try
I don't know why
I don't know why
I try

I try so hard
It's hard to speak
I get so far
For a little piece

Maybe it's just an empty dream
Maybe it's just me

I don't know why
I don't know why
I try
I don't know why
I don't know why
I try

I don't know why
I don't know why
I try

"There's rumours running through these streets, like a windmill in the wind, there's a rumour burning someone's ears, from these wagging chins"

LOST TOGETHER

I started satisfied
With a wind in my sail
Becoming mystified
I tried to find the wholly grail

And the last thing on my mind
The last thing I would find
Was some empty morning
Too far away

When we get lost together
We prey together
We can win together
Without hitting the ground
But when it gets so slow
And it's all breaking down
We can get lost together
It's all so hard on this merry go round

I started alone
And felt I'd ran a mile
But some little angel
Is looking over me with a smile

Always the last thing I find
Some empty morning in my mind
Some empty morning, too far away

Cause when we get lost together
We prey together
We can win together
Without hitting the ground
But when it gets so slow
And it all starts breaking down
We can get lost together
It's all so hard on this merry go round

It's all so hard on this merry go round

IN A MINUTE

Don't suffocate me
In my twisted hands I hold the key
I can take you from this swell
You're frightened I can see
Don't dislocate me
From this bitter pill that we swallow
But you can save me
Can you save yourself dear fellow

And all these colours, ring a bell
All these dreams they feel like hell
And the freshness I forsake
Carries us through this heartache

And carry me from all I see
Cause in a minute I'll be free
In a minute make no mistake
In a minute that's all it take's
In a minute, it's all before you now

There's a hybrid of maniacs
In my street, please
Twisted up maybe
Maybe it's just me
And if this night
Gives you no pleasure
Then I just might
Dance with the devil

And all these colours, ring a bell
All these dreams they feel like hell
And the freshness I forsake
Carries us through this heartache

And carry me from all I see
Cause in a minute I'll be free
In a minute make no mistake
In a minute that's all it takes
In a minute, it's all before you now

Scream Louder

Everybody wants to say something
Everybody wants to lead the way
The most of what I ever wanted
Used to fall in the rain
It seems if you have some doubt
And you want to push me right over
All you got to do is make it clear
And pull the mat from under

I think you've been telling me
Everything I need to know

Your talk is cheap, and when you scream louder
You'll get what you really need
Amongst the pieces of all the doubt
You'll be remembered, when you scream
When you scream loud, when you scream louder

Does it always feel the same
Sinking below this level
Washed away in mistakes
Are there any words that really matter
You could steer me
Little by little down this lane
But I've got a sneaking suspicion
You're not coming back this way

I think you've been telling me
Everything I need to know

Your talk is cheap, and when you scream louder
You'll get what you really need
Amongst the pieces of all the doubt
You'll be remembered, when you scream
When you scream loud, when you scream louder

I should have let you be right
I should have let you escape
I should have let you be right
I should have wished you on your way

"Through the teardrops of rain, comes a smoking billow, true tales fall from hearts, on to sleepy pillows"

Hope In Us All

Sometimes I've felt lost, on many cold winter days
When the sun that was shining, fell another world away
Love was a twisted highway, drifting down a country path
Darkness a falling shadow, that took away the laughs

So give me the fire back, any time because I have reason
To change a thousand memories, if someone would just listen

I'd like to make the dust a river
With a clean blue shore
With some sense of reason
That I don't have to know any more

Cause the good fruit washes
All this bad away
And the clouds in the darkness
Stop the children playing
But there's some hope in our hearts
Some hope that can start with us all
There's some hope in our hearts
Some hope that can start with us all

Looks like this world, is turning loose out of control
And the stars that were once shining, are looking stale and old
Give me some mood back, a simple word without regret
With some sense of believing, a thousand thoughts to forget

I'd like to make the dust a river
With a clean blue shore
With some sense of reason
That I don't have to know any more

Cause the good fruit washes
All this bad away
And the clouds in the darkness
Stop the children playing
But there's some hope in our hearts
Some hope that can start with us all
There's some hope in our hearts
Some hope that can start with us all

EMOTION

My eyes are crawling
Over the curves of your body
A controlled situation
If only you would let me

All these dreams
Count for nothing
Why don't you dream with me
The truth hides falling
Careful when you speak

Contain the energy
Let the wave of explosion
Cover you and me
Let our thoughts run
Like moving traffic
Emotions pour freely
Over you and me
Emotions pour freely
Over you and me

If we keep running
We'll be tired from the work
Diamonds mean nothing
If they fall in the dirt

Separate intentions
With sounds of deceit
Running no-where
Let yourself loose with me

Contain the energy
Let the wave of explosion
Cover you and me
Let our thoughts run
Like moving traffic
Emotions pour freely
Over you and me
Emotions pour freely
Over you and me

Perpetual Devotion

You look at me like there's no tomorrow
I showed you the way time and time again
We did so many things together
Guess sometimes there's always a reminder
It's just the same but there's always an end

We're moving on
In our hearts we know why
Forever only belongs
If you're moving with time

It's emotion, it's not forgotten
Moving through time, it's strong and it's one
And I hold on, while I'm in motion
A deep bond, perpetual devotion
Show me some, perpetual devotion
Perpetual devotion

This black and white street
Has known my name
For so long it led me through time
But now like a statue I'm left standing
Give me some wings to fly me away
It's just the same but there's always an end

We're moving on
In our hearts we know why
Forever only belongs
If you're moving with time

It's emotion, it's not forgotten
Moving through time, it's strong and it's one
And I hold on, while I'm in motion
A deep bond, perpetual devotion
Show me some, perpetual devotion
Perpetual devotion

Perpetual devotion

"If I had a crystal ball to see ahead, I'd tell everyone about themselves"

Richard has amazing musical talent, bringing my words to life endlessly.

Cold Silence

When things go wrong
I look at the stars outside
When something's done
You know you can't turn back time
We lose each other
Between the fire and the flame
With nothing left to show
Just the respect we gained

When we get closer, we get so far away
We sit in the same room, staring out that same old window frame

It's a cold silence, which makes the ice
It's the final stare, which freezes both ends of our lives
And I'm sure this makes us learn
The cold, cold silence
Ruining us too soon
It's called cold silence
Ruining us too soon

It's these moments in the air
That put temptation sharp as a knife
We reach into our hearts for words
That will give us the strength to fight
In the minds of each of us
We hold the cards that make us believe
Within each of us lies hope
In the cold there is a key

When we get closer, we get so far away
We sit in the same room, staring out that same old window frame

It's a cold silence which makes the ice
It's the final stare, which freezes both ends of our lives
And I'm sure this makes us learn
The cold, cold silence
Ruining us too soon
It's called cold silence
Ruining us too soon

DESPERATION

Heard the cry from inside
I get the feeling I've been pushed away
Second sense says you lied to me
You're covering over the footsteps you made

I get the feeling I'm losing
Losing sight of what I used to see
The grip I had is slowly slipping
Sense you are drifting away

And believe me I've been trying
Trying hard to be a saint
But my heart is losing rhythm
Inside I'm starting to bleed

Bleeding out of desperation
The wounds I have don't seem to fade
I feel the love we have been making
Is slowly starting to escape

Moving closer to your lips
Your whispers tell me the truth
With all desperation's agony
In between the dreams we create

There's no use in trying
If only one of us has a plan
There's no use pretending
To offer everything in our hands

And believe me I've been trying
Trying hard to be a saint
But my heart is losing rhythm
Inside I'm starting to bleed

Bleeding out of desperation
The wounds I have don't seem to fade
I feel the love we have been making
Is slowly starting to escape

CRYSTAL GLASS

The sweet success is tender and it's ripe
And when you hold me I don't put up a fight
Are my eyes telling me lies
Simple things that I believed
Simple things that helped me survive

And I am falling further down
You never said that you were coming around
Your blue eyes cut me in half

I handle you like crystal glass
I handle you like crystal glass

Time and time again I stand
In front of you I show my hands
Temptation is hard to resist
Inside I hold no prejudice

And I am falling further down
You never said that you were coming around
Your blue eyes cut me in half

I handle you like crystal glass
I handle you like crystal glass

The memories stay on my mind
They go back to the very first night
All the warmth and a gentle touch
Nothing could ever matter that much

And I am falling further down
You never said that you were coming around
Your blue eyes cut me in half

I handle you like crystal glass
I handle you like crystal glass

"And it confuses me, maybe it's the heat you leave, it's sure not the moon I see, or this rain falling down on me, you're a mystery"

Bourbon Street

Bring your lips a little closer honey
Wet them as cold as an ice block for me
Kissing's become a habit
Since this part of the street closed up

No free drinks are passing through
The lights are dull and dim
Forget about a scotch on the rocks
The door is closed and I can't get in

Now they lock up the hall
And there's just a passing parade
There's nothing to toast
Just an empty glass
And a bottled-up ghost
Down on Bourbon Street

We were promised the world by the DJ
He had us all stuck up
As we listened to the Neville Brothers
Smoke was choking us all up

Now they lock up the hall
And there's just a passing parade
There's nothing to toast
Just an empty glass
And a bottled-up ghost
Down on Bourbon Street
Down on Bourbon Street

Pretending You Know My Name

Never had so many holes in my pockets
The change just keeps on rolling through
I've got enough money to buy me love
Sticks to my fingers like glue

There ain't no use running baby
Like a locomotive off the rails
When it gets too much maybe
You better dig deep and find the wheels

I tell you there ain't no use honey
There ain't no use in praying
When the sun comes up you'll be lonely
Remember last night I was saying

You can't be spoon fed money
You can't hide yourself in the rain
When you're soaking and you're crying
There's no use pretending you know my name

Got to stop pretending
You're one of the gentry type
Lipstick and makeup go a long way
But it won't get you what you want tonight

There ain't no use running baby
Like a locomotive off the rails
When it gets too much maybe
You better dig deep and find the wheels

I tell you there ain't no use honey
There ain't no use in praying
When the sun comes up you'll be lonely
Remember last night I was saying

You can't be spoon fed money
You can't hide yourself in the rain
When you're soaking and you're crying
There's no use pretending you know my name
There's no use pretending you know my name

PREYING FOR LOVE

Have you reached the end of the road tonight
Have you gone and lost the bet
Have you hidden behind a closed door
With your face soaking and wet

Have you gone and played your last card
When you answered with a yes
Did you hide behind a face called love
How did you fix the mess

And girl there are reasons, for you there are none
When you took the measures to cover up love

Now you're preying for love
Now you're killing time
Trying to get it together
What it feels deep down inside
Well sure there's some hope in there
But sometimes it's not enough
Then you get the knives out
And you'd kill and prey for love

Have you found another way tonight
Have you faced the truth and left
Have you felt the fire burning
How did you leave an empty bed

And girl there are reasons, for you there are none
When you took the measures to cover up love

Now you're preying for love
Now you're killing time
Try to get it together
What it feels deep down inside
Well sure there's some hope in there
But sometimes it's not enough
Then you get the knives out
And you'd kill and prey for love

"There's no compromise, there's no in betweens, no half measures, when you don't believe. There's no hint of surrender, when we can't see eye to eye, good things are hard to remember, when there's no compromise"

CRIME CITY

Nighttime falls in a crowded city
A black cat creeps with a bleeding tail
Dices roll on a footpath that is dirty
White flags flicker in a gale

Papers crawl across the street
Wrecking balls knock old buildings down
Time is the motion to beat
In the distance you will hear the sounds

Of screaming mothers
And crying babies
Fighting fathers
Trying to save them
It's such a pity
This is a crime city
No trace is left of man

They say a bullet doesn't have any name on it
But there's no mercy on who
It chooses to hit
One hope dies on a timeless dream
When man's free and no-one chases him

You hear screaming mothers
And crying babies
Fighting fathers
Trying to save them
It's such a pity
This is a crime city
No trace is left of man

OUR OWN EYES

Tonight we seen an angel calling
Tonight our wings are spread across the sky
Tonight the stars cry like us
Just like our own eyes

And our tears are wet like some holy water
Our tears wet the morning dust
Tonight, how can we ever forget
The night we found more than love

And now I see the proof in you
Now I hear your cries
Warm and soft like a gentle touch
Has let us see it
With our own eyes

Enriched inside my mind I carried hope
Inside this soul I'm so engraved
The sky above let us see the rope
Together we are saved

And our tears are wet like some holy water
Our tears wet the morning dust
Tonight, how can we ever forget
The night we found more than love

And now I see the proof in you
Now I hear your cries
Warm and soft like a gentle touch
Has let us see it
With our own eyes

And now I find the truth in you
Lost in the disguise
Warm just like our gentle hearts
Has let us see it
Has let us see it
With our own eyes

ELAINE

I must have looked a sorry man
When I turned another page
Between this book I lost my way
I lost you inside this maze

But the greyness of some hope lives on
And the trust we had survives
Forget about the rain that's here
Let me wipe the tears from your eyes

The cold nights knocked on our door
I was afraid to open up
To speak my mind was a matter of words
I couldn't conjure up

Now there is an open door
That leads me to your heart
Through these streets of hope I found
Your open heart ready for love

Elaine we're free from the winter
We're free from all the rain
Your voice has soothed this aching heart
And let me start again
Elaine we're free from this winter
Three seasons has left us pain
I was cold but that was yesterday
We're back where we should be Elaine

Elaine

The man I wrote my first ever lyric and song with, Kev Farley.

"It's an old lesson, it's an old part, there are no reasons, just listen to your heart"

BLUES IN MY VEINS

Every night I sleep I dream
About the things I used to do
The nightmares are few and far between
When I remember you
We used to call every night
At the local drinking den
Dancing and singing
With every one of our friends

And everything's changing now
As much as the sun goes down
The same faces stare into the mirrors
They're just doing other things out of town

The shadows fall then it rains
I've still got the blues in my veins
The night falls I pull the reins
I've still got the blues
I've still got the blues in my veins

Walking these streets I'm all alone
Reading every street sign
The mist below my feet
Is taking me back in time
The cigar smell drifts
From behind those big red doors
I can't hear the numbers any more
The tone of the sax is gone

And everything's changing now
As much as the sun goes down
The same faces stare into the mirrors
They're just doing other things out of town

The shadows fall then it rains
I've still got the blues in my veins
The night falls I pull the reins
I've still got the blues
I've still got the blues, in my veins

DON'T LET IT GO TONIGHT

I saw you creeping through the darkness
I had the light on my side
I caught your eye from the corner of the door
As you tried to be precise

I know you tried to keep the windows open
But the wind keeps howling through this place
And I know what you're trying to do
I know that look on your face

Don't let it go tonight
Don't let the foundations fall
Just pick up the pieces
From where we left off
I don't want to see you fall
Don't let it go tonight

You speak with a constant tongue
You've been obsessed by our love
Now we reach out to find an empty hand
Seems a lost soul is not enough

I know you tried to let me know before
The best ways that you could
But I can't see the sense in saying
Be my wolf come out of the woods

Don't let it go tonight
Don't let the foundations fall
Just pick up the pieces
From where we left off
I don't want to see you fall
Don't let it go tonight
Don't let it go tonight

LOVE ENDS WITH A WHISPER

Love ends with a whisper
Love ends with a lonely word
Between the softness of cold skin
Between the words unheard

Love ends with a whisper
Time heals the wounds
No-one ever listens
To how it really hurts

Love begins in an instant
Love falls from the moon
To someone who's innocent
It all begins too soon

In a whisper
It's a whisper
It's an innocent tune
Graced in between loneliness
They say it's only for fools

In a whisper
It's a whisper
There are no rules
Love ends with a whisper
Love ends and it's cruel

Words only half tell
The secrets that you make
Love can end with a whisper
Whispers of heartbreak

In a whisper
It's a whisper
There are no rules
Love ends with a whisper
Love ends and it's cruel

"And don't you try to tell me, don't you try to bend me now, I'm on the edge, walking eggshells, and you're pushing me I'm falling down"

Don't Go Losing Hope

Someone's out to get you
Someone's blowing smoke
Someone's driving through your street
But don't go losing
Don't go losing hope

The more they try and catch you
The more they fall away
The more they try and tease you
The more a man has to pay
So don't go losing
Don't go losing hope

Don't go losing
Don't go losing hope

And I don't want to see you
Losing any sight
Of the kind of loving
You're chasing through the night
So don't go losing
Don't go losing hope

Don't go losing
Don't go losing hope
Don't go losing
Don't go losing hope

WHILE THE CITY SLEEPS

Darkness falls across the street
The night is closing in
Barking dogs howl down the cars
Not everyone believes what they have seen

When it's after hours
And the shopping doors are closed
Run the streets of emptiness
Dancing like nobody knows

While the city sleeps
Some little angel mends our hearts
While the city dreams
Some little angel mends our scars
Beneath our feet
Some little angel sets our paths
While the city sleeps
Some little angel mends our hearts

Electricity of lights
Blink like a camera lens
Through the windows streets are stained
With crazy stories that never end

And if it gets too much
Someone's not far from your reach
When the days get so tough
Dance like you never did

While the city sleeps
Some little angel mends our hearts
While the city dreams
Some little angel mends our scars
Beneath our feet
Some little angel sets our paths
While the city sleeps
Some little angel mends our hearts

While the city sleeps
Some little angel mends our hearts

SALVATION

Looking down a long hallway
Open doors and empty smiles
Tried to walk through a moment
So many times I could have lied
I don't like where I've been
Sure seems real lost now
Never once you listened to me
You don't know how much I tried

I don't know how to get it back
I don't know how to live on rations
Maybe all we need is time
And a little more salvation
A little more than a human trap
Maybe give into temptation
Maybe all I need is a map
And a little more salvation

It's so close now I feel it
Funny how emotion slips through
Seems some time has passed now
And there lies the shadow of truth
I don't know where I've been
Sure seems real bad now
Never once you counted on me
You don't know how much I tried

I don't know how to get it back
I don't know how to live on rations
Maybe all we need is time
And a little more salvation
A little more than a human trap
Maybe give into temptation
Maybe all I need is a map
And a little more salvation

Seems a little frustrating to me
Seems a little offline to you
Maybe all I need is a map
And a little more salvation

"Tell me how you see me, and I'll tell you how I see you, you're always the breath inside of me, that brings out the truth"

Always thinking of new lyrical hooks.

WHERE I WANNA BE

Feel it going down slowly
Like the sun behind a lonely hill
Like my faults falling one by one
Nothing seems to give me the thrill

Feel it like an ocean breeze
Drifting like a full moon across the park
Reflecting like emotions in the sun
Feels like it hits real hard

And I can't see because it's clouded
And it's never really any fun
But where I want to be is here
Not going down like a ton
Cause it's falling one by one
Where I want to be is facing me
And in front of me those dreams I find
Will go on and on and on

My hearts tied I know it's tight
But the strings are not attached
Like a fire I once fought within me
I followed the right path, the right map

And I can't see because it's past
And it's never really any fun
But where I want to be is here
Not going down like a ton
Cause it's falling one by one
Where I want to be is facing me
And in front of me those dreams I find
Will go on and on and on

WOULD YOU

Would you still love me, if sometimes I was all wrong
Would you still love me, even if I couldn't hold on
Would you still love me, if I was always pulling away
Would you still know me, just as much as you did yesterday

Would you still love me, if I was cold, and become faded
Would you still love me, if I become lost and jaded
And would you keep loving me, if I turned and never believed
In a moment of helpless truth, would you still shelter me

And would you still love me, if the grip becomes so loose
If I had to do something, that wasn't totally the truth
And would you still love me, for all and who that I am
If I was blind and I hurt you, would you still believe that we can

And would you ever push me, if I hurt you mistakenly
And would you keep loving me, if accidentally I fell heavily
And would you still love me, if the sky was no longer blue
And in a moment of doubt
Would I be replaced with someone new

And would you still love me
For all and who that I am
Would you still love me, unconditionally
And would you still love me
For all and who that I am
Would you still love me
Would you still believe that we can

ALL ABOARD

She woke one morning at the train stop
Time had passed and dreams had faded
She knew now it was the last cut
That she could never be what he created

He was cold and he knew why
It was another hand dealt with fate
The night was edged with a clear sign
Both too young, too little, too late

They don't want to be cruel, they don't want to be kind
They've got to find out, what's next in their lives

And she waves slowly, turns her head right around
Forgets the enemy, the man that pulled her down
He falls heavily, remembers the night she called
Three stairs from the platform, this time it's all aboard

Another day waits down the railway line
Mile by mile the mist disappears
Just a little more time and a week away
The dust will settle and the road will be clear

He's got to find another man inside
Deep within the one he doesn't know
A lost soul has been touched
Can he rise above the words she yelled

They don't want to be cruel, they don't want to be kind
They've got to find out, what's next in their lives

And she waves slowly, turns her head right around
Forgets the enemy, the man that pulled her down
He falls heavily, remembers the night she called
Three stairs from the platform, this time it's all aboard

"And I know one day we'll get it right, we'll knock down the walls that stop us, that remain so tough and tight. We'll follow a way that in the end just won't burn us, grab a feeling of winning and being something, when the heart matters"

My Hurt

Ride the subway at night
You'll see faces that make up the world
Between the seats are dreams
We all reach for but we can't hold

Take a trip to no-where
A room that has no lights
Between the pages are tears
A heart that has no fight

That's my hurt
Feel's like digging in the dirt
That's my hurt
That's my hurt, that I live with

I hear every sound around me
Sometimes touches deep
And the life I lived I believed
But I still can't find my feet

That's my hurt
Feel's like digging in the dirt
That's my hurt
That's my hurt, that I live with

And where's the world of trust
Where's the world divine
On a soul boat, on a soul boat
We are all trying to find

That's my hurt
Feel's like digging in the dirt
That's my hurt
That's my hurt, that I live with

That's my hurt
Feel's like digging in the dirt
That's my hurt
That's my hurt, we all live with

OUT OF MY DEPTH

Feels like I'm going in circles
Asking questions in my mind
Feels like some direction
I just can't find

Going in deeper I hide
Because I know I'm the one
That needs to pull
These strings undone

I'm out of my depth
I'm not breathing
I'm not proud
I'm out of my depth
Taking little steps
Feels like drowning
On the ground

Feels like I committed some crime
I lost focus and I believed
All the nice things, you've been telling me

I'm out of my depth
I'm not breathing
I'm not proud
I'm out of my depth
Taking little steps
Feels like drowning
On the ground

And the world keeps turning all around me
But I'm still learning, how to find my feet

I'm out of my depth
I'm not breathing
I'm not proud
I'm out of my depth
Taking little steps
Feels like drowning
On the ground

What's Going On

She says what's going on
What's coming around this time
She says she's sick of the days
I keep her holding on and waiting in line
Maybe I should take a ride
To the end of this street
She says she should have stayed and played me
Took a little off her feet

She says what's going on
Did I come around at the wrong time
Should I just be me, should I make her believe
What's on my mind
And all the things going on
All the things going on, at this time

You say you've been let down
But I didn't mean to commit no crime
Asking questions that make no sense
Rubbing out the sand that marks the line

She says what's going on
Did I come around at the wrong time
Should I just be me, should I make her believe
What's on my mind
And all the things going on
All the things going on, at this time

These pictures don't remind me
They just take me on a journey

She says what's going on
Did I come around at the wrong time
Should I just be me, should I make her believe
What's on my mind
And all the things going on
All the things going on, at this time

"And I want to believe everything you ever told me, I want it to last forever, I want to believe everything you ever told me, just like the way you showed me"

THAT'S JUST WHAT HAPPENS

There are so many ways to count the costs
There are so many ways to hear a song
Between a man and a woman feelings get lost
But there are some things that help you along

Sometimes it's just a puzzle
Sometimes a great big haze
Stuck between two worlds in trouble
We'd like to wish for better days

But it's sane, it's just a game

That's just what happens
That's just what happens
To you and me anyway

You tell me you'd wait sometimes
For some hope in your promised life
It's just another game we play
Some things are too late to get right

Sometimes it takes patience
Sometimes mistakes are made
That's what you get in relation
When the foundations have been laid

But it's sane, it's just a game

That's just what happens
That's just what happens
To you and me anyway

The standards are high, problem is I'm far too low
That's just what happens, when there's no-where else to go

That's just what happens
That's just what happens
To you and me anyway

IGNITE

I feel like I'm cruising
Down some broken highway
Alone without something
I think I've had better days

I feel like I'm humming
There's so much I used to know
It starts to feel like nothing
I've got nothing left to show

I feel like I'm drifting
Alone through some blue sky
Touching some cloud
That's bringing hope to my mind

There's nothing to grab
Just a load of honesty
Just a feeling inside
That's trying to break free

Let's break this stone, let's see what's inside
Maybe some fun, maybe some fight
Let's break this skin, and bleed it all dry
There's some hope in here, about to ignite

I feel like busting
The cause in two halves
Pushing and lifting
I'm like a broken-down car

And like a slow-moving train
I'm left in this jam, it's never the same
An open mind, an open hand

Let's break this stone, let's see what's inside
Maybe some fun, maybe some fight
Let's break this bone, and bleed it all dry
There's some hope in here, about to ignite

TIME TO BE ME

Packed my bags I'm leaving
Been wrestling these thoughts too long
Stood on the highest mountain, saw it all
Time to get a little strong

Follow my dream down stream
Find a place that's all me
It's taken so long to get here
You've got to realise I want to be complete

It's time to be me, it's time to move on
Time to let go, all that was wrong
It's time to be me, it's time to push on
But can I have your shoulder
Just in case I need something to lean on

Seems it takes a lifetime
To build your dreams inside
Sometimes I lost all my strength
Felt I wanted to give up the fight

But now I know me
And if I want to believe
I got to be the one to show you
You changed me, I want to be complete

It's time to be me, it's time to move on
Time to let go, all that was wrong
It's time to be me, it's time to push on
But can I have your shoulder
Just in case I need something to lean on

Packed my bags I'm leaving
Been wrestling these thoughts too long
Stood on the highest mountain, screamed it
Time to get a little strong

It's time to be me, it's time to move on

"Don't cry tonight, save the words you want to hear, for someone who is lonely, by the loneliness of fear. Don't cry tonight, it's just a lonely world, where teardrops rain down, on every little girl"

Many of my lyrics have been written in this very chair.

Hurt Me Breaking The Rules

I can hear the thunder coming
A cloud hangs inside this room
Your motors always running
I run for cover before you start to move

You said you'd be a lady
But now I see the truth
Your motors always stalling
You're trying to run me over
Before you start to move

You hurt me with your promise
You hurt me with your spite
With the rope you tied you bound me
You hurt me with your lies
You hurt me down deep inside
Now I'm just the fool
Choking at the throat you hold me
You hurt me breaking the rules

You walked into your own trap
You set it with your doubt
Now you leave me empty
Then you push me all about

You walked into your own slap
Now you're bleeding from the mouth
I'm not your puppet on a string
That you can gently push about

You hurt me with your promise
You hurt me with your spite
With the rope you tied you bound me
You hurt me with your lies
You hurt me down deep inside
Now I'm just the fool
Choking at the throat you hold me
You hurt me breaking the rules

You Defy Me

Piece of mind drifts over me
My defenses crumble
When I'm in your company
Everything you do
You do for a reason
Excuses fall into my lap
And it's teasing, when you defy me

When you defy me
Everything changes
You cried to me
And wet the pages
The writing fades
And it's harder to see
If you ever wanted
To satisfy me, when you defy me

When you defy me
I'm scratching my head
Words spoken softly
Drift off my bed
When you defy me
Everything you said falls away
Knowing that you lied to me
Hurts the most inside, when you defy me

Existence is what I'm suffering
In my heart it's an open fence
I'm going back to where I've been
I might just find another chance
When you defy me

When you defy me
I'm scratching my head
Words spoken softly
Drift off my bed
When you defy me
Everything you said falls away
Knowing that you lied to me
Hurts the most inside, when you defy me

WORDS I'VE NEVER SPOKEN

The blue sky's dawning through my window
A bright light shines on your face
Sweet smells give me a hint of you
Words tangle up in your embrace

And all this lipstick is mistaken
You're warmer than I've ever known
There's a true woman's scent in the air
Words linger that I've never outgrown

And there's a fire
A little flame
The proof drowns in your lust
The silent letters in your name
Fingertips and a gentle touch
I search for an opening
A silent word a little praise
You're lost between the words I've never spoken

There's a fire burning inside me
I'm trying not to feel like steel
The air I breathe suffocates me
And never feels quite real

You stand like a memory inside me
And after the smoke has cleared
There's still some hope inside me
Drowning in the words I feared

And there's a fire
A little flame
The proof drowns in your lust
The silent letters in your name
Fingertips and a gentle touch
I search for a moment
A silent word a little praise
You're lost between the words
I've never spoken

"Is this where the wind blows, when it's over, is it time to take another look around. Is this where the wind blows, when it's over, when hearts that are soft pound. Is this where the wind blows, when it's over"

Fight On The Outside

Every night of my life I'm left standing
Like a creature I've just landed
Trying to find my way through winter
After three seasons have already hit you

Every night I bow to my lover
Leave all the boys to celebrate with mother nature
Drinking till they want to lie down and die
My girlfriend says it's alright to be with her
I want to know who's telling me lies

It's a fight
It's a fight on the outside
Every night inside it's killing me
Leave me butterflies to fly me through
Cut all the strings untie me now
Cut all the ropes that bind me down
Seems I spend my whole life fighting with you
On the inside
I fight on the outside too

Open your arms you can hold me tight
Tell me something that will calm me down
Give me some sign through this window
Something good to spend my time around

The boys are out or didn't I tell you
I'm looking for something else to spend time on
Something better than loving can do
Something more that will make me strong

It's a fight
It's a fight on the outside
Every night inside it's killing me
Leave me butterflies to fly me through
Cut all the strings untie me now
Cut all the ropes that bind me down
Seems I spend my whole life fighting with you
On the inside
I fight on the outside too

THE FUTURE'S CHANGING THE PAST

Hands of time can't be turned back
But you can mend the broken strings
You just need to take off the slack
And forget about everything
Your memory will slowly fade now
Push all the reasons aside
Let the candle you've been holding
Slowly dim the light

Then in the nighttime
You can leave your shadow fast
You can pray in the nighttime
The future's changing the past

Let it be a memory
End the bad dreams they will pass
Take the future in your hands
Cause the future's changing the past
Let it be a victory
The bad dreams they don't last
Take the future in your hands
Cause the future's changing the past

You don't have to have a reason
The fire inside you will scare the ghost
You can change with every silly season
In the end you'll be the first past the post
Then in the nighttime
You can sail, put up your mast
You can pray in the nighttime
The future's changing the past

Let it be a memory
End the bad dreams they will pass
Take the future in your hands
Cause the future's changing the past
Let it be a victory
The bad dreams they don't last
Take the future in your hands
Cause the future's changing the past

HURRICANE

Tonight the arrows swaying
Like a pendulum out of control
Like a rock we're sinking slowly
In a love out of the cold

There's a cloud hanging over us baby
The hot sun is fading fast
Some things have to come together
If this dream is going to last

We're torn between two lovers
Torn between the pain
When the lightning comes from above
Nothing will be saved
We're torn between two lovers
Standing in the rain
Trying to hide some broken faith
Standing in a hurricane

Heard about love on the rocks
Heard about a Romeo in Spain
Juliet was an angel that's no secret
It's no secret that was a play

Now we're looking down a barrel
Of a hundred different guns
Staring in the face of danger
Staring at an ex loved one

We're torn between two lovers
Torn between the pain
When the lightning comes from above
Nothing will be saved
We're torn between two lovers
Standing in the rain
Trying to hide some broken faith
Standing in a hurricane

"Now I'm sleeping with a nightmare, a black dream that makes me scared, I'm reaching for something to hold, only finding an empty bed. I'm trying to mend these wounds, I'm a ghost without a soul, and I'm trying to fix this heart, this heart with a thousand holes"

Make Believe

Saw a saddle on a strange horse
Walking along a side street
Saw a cradle with a baby
Living in a foundry

Saw a maid in a dark room
Who could never keep her feet
Saw a man lost and empty
With his dreams set in concrete

Have you ever seen the same things
Have you ever had the same dreams
Were they all the real things
Or was it make believe
Did they rise from the same seeds
The seeds that set us free
Were they all the real things
Or was it make believe

Saw a girl with an open shirt
Running along the sand
Took a trip to Frankfurt
Somewhere I lost the plan

Saw a star fall after midnight
It crashed into my hands
Caught a small boat to China
But never made it off the land

Have you ever seen the same things
Have you ever had the same dreams
Were they all the real things
Or was it make believe
Did they rise from the same seeds
The seeds that set us free
Were they all the real things
Or was it make believe

BALLAD OF SURPRISE

It's no surprise
You look at me that way
It's almost like I tore your heart out
It's so sublime
The words you have to say
You couldn't try any harder

I took away
Everything we ever had
You said you needed something more
Never felt it got that bad
But I guess it happens when everything starts to fall

Then we left, the things unsaid
Then we left, the things undone
Then we left, the things unsaid
Then we left, the things undone

I've looked down deep
From so far up
I'm still trying to work it out from here
You remind me of
A sunrise in the mist
Something that never got that near

It's all compromised
And when it all comes to shore
It's like a dream that comes floating back
And when it's too late to turn around
Each burning door comes swinging cracked

Then we left, the things unsaid
Then we left, the things undone
Then we left, the things unsaid
Then we left, the things undone

Ballad of surprise

TELL ME

I see your eyes, reflecting in the mirror
I can tell that you're looking for some kind of hero
Most of us know, how this wind can change
But how do we stop this hunger, how do we stop this rain

And I watch you, and I know you
You're everything I'd like to be
And I want you to see, the same in me

Tell me how you see me
And I'll tell you how I see you
You're always the breath inside of me
That brings out the truth
Tell me how you see me
I'll tell you how I see you
Do I keep you standing
And your life complete

I've dreamed of running
And flying over every mountain
I've often thought and wondered
If you feel the same way about it

And I watch you, and I know you
You're everything I'd like to be
And I want you to see, the same in me

Tell me how you see me
And I'll tell you how I see you
You're always the breath inside of me
That brings out the truth
Tell me how you see me
I'll tell you how I see you
Do I keep you standing
And your life complete

Tell me how you see me

Some things really are cool. Like Harvey and his studio, where we have written many songs together here.

"I see a madman on the loose, today I seen the axe fall. Mother Nature strikes again, it's the calm before the storm"

FEELING LONELY

Sitting by the water
Feeling overcrowded
I should have known
All about it

Feeling lonely
Feeling lonely

Watching everybody
Talking, walking away
Watching what could have been
Drifting away

Feeling lonely
Feeling lonely

I feel the ice air
Coming inside of me
Finding it hard to breathe
There is a memory
That could take me where
You could be
That could make me bare
All for you to see

Feeling lonely
Feeling lonely

Does it matter
That I can't see
The weathered faces
In front of me

Does it matter
Feeling lonely
Feeling lonely
Does it matter
Feeling lonely

FAMILY

I see this familiar light, up on the family tree
Shining all around me, there's a warmth embracing me
Like dreaming of flying, together all through life
The fun and the understanding, little devils into adult life

And we watch and we serve each other
Comforting in the night
We grow up, helping each other
Through each other's life

And it's right what they say
The true meaning of family
Is held amongst every feeling
A hug, a shake, a kiss
We share each other's dream
We move through life happily
The true meaning that it brings
 In a family

There's nothing so sure, when you hear the voices outside
About to be wrapped in arms, full of memories and shared life
Our blood is like a river, flowing from each other to the shore
It's in your skin, it's in your heart, it's everything and more

And we watch and we serve each other
Comforting in the night
We grow up, helping each other
Through each other's life

And it's right what they say
The true meaning of family
Is held amongst every feeling
A hug, a shake, a kiss
We share each other's dream
We move through life happily
The true meaning that it brings
In a family

Heart On My Sleeve

I'd bleed for you
I'd keep all your secrets
I'd heal any wounds
Hurt souls are the deepest
I'd hold you closer
Than anyone ever could
I'd be your summer
If the cool winds were blowing through

I know you, and you better believe
What's old and what's new
I wear my heart on my sleeve
I'm there for you
My hearts there for keeps
I'm there for you
I wear my heart on my sleeve

Love doesn't get lost easy
Love just doesn't get found
But some places love
Just seems to hang around
There's a place real close
It's not too far away
Between these weathered arms
You'll find warmth goes without saying

I know you, and you better believe
What's old and what's new
I wear my heart on my sleeve
I'm there for you
My hearts there for keeps
I'm there for you
I wear my heart on my sleeve

Love doesn't get lost easy
Love just doesn't get found
But some places love
Just seems to hang around

"Take the pictures off the wall, you can leave the frames, cause I'll be going back, going back someday. Just hide the windowpanes, with some curtains from the rain, because I'll be going back, I'll be going home someday"

My Day Has Come

Morning breaks the skyline
Once again my eyes are red
I drag myself over, and out of bed
It's on again, never seems to end
Seems I crash into walls
Everywhere I go, I bet it shows
Must look like I've been crying
You hit me low, the hurt must show

I don't know if you feel the same
But I'm not here to blame

Because my day has come
What followed me was wrong
My life has changed, my mind is strong
Yesterday is gone, tomorrow is on
My day has come

I am stronger now
I've learn't to love myself, forgive myself, everyone else
I've been moving forward
Breaking away, I'm having better days

I don't know if you feel the same
But I'm not here to blame

Because my day has come
What followed me was wrong
My life has changed, my mind is strong
Yesterday is gone, tomorrow is on
My day has come

And you might feel like moving closer
And if it looks that way, I'll turn you over
Cause I don't feel the same
I'm not here to blame

My day has come

All That Remains

See the light, shining down from up above
See the love, reaching out for something new
See the sky, clouding all that makes you weak
Must be trust that will make you start to believe

Now all that remains
Are the stains of something old
Don't try to change
It's so hard to keep a hold
When you lose that faith
And you can't cut those chains
There's just a shadow
In all that remains

Feel the breeze, it makes you weak inside
And the warmth, is everything you need to find
It will show, when it comes from time to time
You will know, when the time is really right

Now all that remains
Are the stains of something old
Don't try to change
It's so hard to keep a hold
When you lose that faith
And you can't cut those chains
There's just a shadow
In all that remains

Now turn it all around, forget the calling pain
Come someday, today, is all that remains

In all that remains
Are the stains of something old
Don't try to change
It's so hard to keep a hold
When you lose that faith
And you can't cut those chains
There's just a shadow
In all that remains

My Breath

How do I know I'm alive
And you are beside me
How do I show you
I'm blinded without being silent

How do I trust you
When this world fades to grey
How do I know you
Won't be my fate

Tell me you'll be my breath
You'll be my rock, my rain
Tell me you'll be my breath
And our breaths will be the same

How do I be patient
When I want something fast
How will I know you are close to me
You're not too far

How do I preserve
My beating bleeding heart
When I am mourning
When we're far apart

Tell me you'll be my breath
You'll be my rock, my rain
Tell me you'll be my breath
And our breaths will be the same

Tell me you'll be my breath
You'll be my air, my flame
Tell me you'll be my breath
And our breaths will be the same
Will be the same

Tell me you'll be my breath
And our breaths will be the same

BURNT OUT

I feel so lost inside
Surprised by everything
Never knowing what's behind
Is going to change the way I think
I feel so dark and hide
Between every lonely wall inside
All I seem to find
Is no relief and in my core

I'm bleeding and I'm old
I'm falling and I'm cold
There's nothing that can change the way I feel
I need hope to get me through all of this
I need love to get me through all of this
I need you to get me through all of this
Just hold me close
To your heart

I know it doesn't matter
To a heart that's torn and blackened
It feels all loose and tattered
I've become so ashened from all of this
I fell on a lonely sword
All I do is cry myself to sleep
And all I do is wonder why
There's no relief and in my world

I'm bleeding and I'm old
I'm falling and I'm cold
There's nothing that can change the way I feel
I need hope to get me through all of this
I need love to get me through all of this
I need you to get me through all of this
Just hold me close
To your heart

It feels so empty, believe me it all hurts
I give myself whole to you now
There's still so far we have to go
When it's burnt and falling down

In the studio with Richard, Shannon Jackson and Stuart Johnson. Some of my fondest work has been with and for Schism the band.

"In your eyes, I see time fly, through my fingers, the frost bites. You walk slowly, shed your skin, you're light years, from letting me in"

REASONS

You wake me up inside
You capture my heart
You bring me to life
You're the light in my dark
You're everything to me
My strength in the storm
You hold me as I dream
We are safe, we are warm

You whisper the words that hold me together
You bring me the stars that fall down from heaven

You're all the reasons, I have love inside
You're all the reasons that I can fly
You help me to stand when I'm falling
When I'm crying you wipe my eyes
You're all the reasons that I'm alive

You are the shade I seek
In the heat of the day
You hold me when I'm weak
You make it all okay
You touch me deep within
Warm me when I'm cold
I feel your breath on my skin
You keep me young when I'm old

You whisper the words that hold us together
You make me feel, like I'm in heaven

You're all the reasons, I have love inside
You're all the reasons that I can fly
You help me to stand when I'm falling
When I'm crying you wipe my eyes
You're all the reasons that I'm alive

Too many to count, but I'm sure going give it a try
Even if it takes forever, I'll be telling you why
You're all the reasons that I'm alive

TOGETHER WE CAN SHINE

Take a hand
Take a stand
Take a step for certainty
Rise and shine
For a day
When we care for unity

Climate change
Ease the strain
For our city our families
All as one
We are strong
Together in harmony

Don't waste this time
Enrich this world
Hear our voice
It can be heard
There's a choice
Yours and mine
And together
We can shine

Time for change
Time to plan
Walk together on this land
Time to trust
What we must
Together hand in hand

Don't waste this time
Enrich this world
Hear our voice
It can be heard
There's a choice
Yours and mine
And together
We can shine

Together we can shine

Seeds of Songs

At First Light

Do you think you could be
The first one to see me
At first light
Through the night
You must need love

Do you feel
You could bleed
All of your time for me
Or keep me on my knees
With the promises you promise me

At first light
Can I be your first touch
The one that you see
At first light
Can I be the one that you reach
The one that you need
At first light, at first light

Will you fade
Between the night
Will the stars show the way
I'm here now
Will you stay strong
When the day breaks

Can you wait another moment
Something good may come along
I don't know what I'd do alone
If I had to stay here and stay strong

At first light
Can I be your first touch
The one that you see
At first light
Can I be the one that you reach
The one that you need
At first light, at first light

YOU'RE HERE NOW

When you know that it gets tough, move closer to me
I'm there next to you, I feel you believe
There's plenty of time left, it's all right
There's more of you I crave, your inside

My heart now
Come on throw your arms down
Only we can understand, feeling this way
In our hands now
Time feels like an eternity
Our souls maybe tied and bound
But our hearts keep saying
You're here now

Don't think about it too much, we can build it up again
Just look at all this distance, as a brand-new beginning
There's plenty of time left, it's all right
There's more of you I crave, your inside

My heart now
Come on throw your arms down
Only we can understand, feeling this way
In our hands now
Time feels like an eternity
Our souls maybe tied and bound
But our hearts keep saying
You're here now

Come a little further this time
We can both make it, your inside
Come a little closer it's all right
There's more of you I crave, your inside

My heart now

SOME REASON NOW

You say I don't need to
Carry the weight of the world right now
I don't know where I'm supposed to go
Do I hold on and stay down low

I count a hundred reasons
All you feel you don't believe
Should I surrender to this moment
Or bend to all your needs

Hold on, hold strong
Let's talk about it now
I could listen to every word you say
I could fall but now I doubt it
Hold on, hold strong
Let's both think of all we found
You could be my savior
I could be braver
If you would give me some reason now

Come on try to wait
The sun might come shining through
Catch every tiny raindrop
That's falling down on me and you

That could be enough
But I'm not too sure how it flows
Surrounded by a little hurt inside
It's not so easy to let it go

Hold on, hold strong
Let's talk about it now
I could listen to every word you say
I could fall but now I doubt it
Hold on, hold strong
Let's both think of all we found
You could be my savior
I could be braver
If you would give me some reason now

"I'm caught in the rain, I'm caught in the fire, there's no in betweens, when you're walking a wire. I'm caught in the rain, I'm caught in the fire, there's no in betweens, when you're trying to fly higher"

My brother Craig, a talented musician, performer and actor after one of his shows. He is always giving me lyrical ideas and inspiration.

STRANDED HEART

I looked at you, you looked at me
I could feel something in the breeze
I never thought that you could leave me
Feeling this much at ease

Forever crossed my mind
Does it cross yours at times
Does it cross, does it cross

So much to do, so much to say
This time I won't be running away
I get so scared, I might fall apart
Now help me
Help this stranded heart

I was down, I was out
I'm sure that it's in the past
You picked me up, you gave me love
I just hope it's all enough

Forever crossed my mind
Does it cross yours at times
Does it cross, does it cross

So much to do, so much to say
This time I won't be running away
I get so scared, I might fall apart
Now help me
Help this stranded heart
Now help me
Help this stranded heart

Sometimes it was just a game we play
But I don't want it to be the same
Forever crossed my mind
Does it cross yours at times
Sometimes it was just a game we played
Does it cross yours at times
Now help me help this stranded heart

YESTERDAY'S NEWS

I'm not one for waiting
Like a fall girl in the night
And I'm not one for holding
Something that isn't right
I'm not contemplating
I'm a shadow of the proof
And I won't pay you attention
The time has come and you lose

You had a choice, you had to choose
You're one of the boys
You're yesterday's news
You made a noise, you had to prove
You're one of the boys
You're yesterday's news

I'm not one for claiming
Any prizes that come for free
And I told you from the start
It takes a lot to get my key
So take your treasure chest
Pack your heart up all tight
My doors no longer open
You lost out big time

You had a choice, you had to choose
You're one of the boys
You're yesterday's news
You made a noise, you had to prove
You're one of the boys
You're yesterday's news
I tell you, you're yesterday's news

Don't come running back to me
Crawling, knocking at my door
I've seen it all before
I've seen it all before now
You're yesterday's news

REMEMBER

Does it feel too much to bear right now
Does it feel like you want to run away
Fall on your knees and cry
Does it seem a little too much to hide
Does it feel too much to bury
Holding on against the tide

Remember, surrender
All that we said
Remember, surrender
Together there's an end in sight
When we both have that feeling
We're not going down without a fight

Does it feel like a moment stopped in time
When it flies right over you
And you're holding on inside
Does it seem to fall like rain
And when you try to clear your head
It gets a little cloudy inside again

Remember, surrender
All that we said
Remember, surrender
Together there's an end in sight
When we both have that feeling
We're not going down without a fight

Promise me you'll never go too far
You'll never be the one losing hope
When it's all said and done
You will be the one, the heart I hold

Remember, surrender
All that we said
Remember, surrender
Together there's an end in sight
When we both have that feeling
We're not going down without a fight

STIR CRAZY

I need to get it right
Travel this bumpy road
Turn on the headlights
Take off the load
There's a little further to go
Another moment in time
Knock down all these walls
That keep me chained tonight

I need a little push
I'm on the edge of a knife
Fighting self-doubt, I'm hungrier this time
I need a little rush, that's what it's all about
And I can't help to think
I'm stir crazy now

I need a little more hope
Some strength I can't deny
When nothing else brings me down
I'll be alright

I need a little push
I'm on the edge of a knife
Fighting self-doubt, I'm hungrier this time
I need a little rush, that's what it's all about
And I can't help to think
I'm stir crazy now

I see a new beginning
Another road I'm going down
And I see the good times coming
And nothing's going to stop me
Nothing's going to stop me now

I need a little push
I'm on the edge of a knife
Fighting self-doubt, I'm hungrier this time
I need a little rush, that's what it's all about
And I can't help to think
I'm stir crazy now

ENOUGH ABOUT LOVE

How do I know I'm right
When you're beside me now
How do I show my hands
When I'm blinded inside and out
Will I ever know the truth
Will I ever hold the trust
Do I know enough about you
Do I know enough about love

Everything about us both
Is more than we could choose
How can I move forward now
When in the past I lose

Tell me you'll be my breath
Tell me you'll be my gain
I'm the one you won't forget
Our breaths will be the same
When the world shuts us out
Will I always be that tough
Do I know enough about you
Do I know enough about love

How do I know I'm right
That you'll never walk away
Like all the hope I hold
Like our hearts beat the same
How will I move forward
When I'm holding all the past
I want to believe this warmth
Is always going to last

Tell me you'll be my breath
Tell me you'll be my gain
I'm the one you won't forget
Our breaths will be the same
When the world shuts us out
Will I always be that tough
Do I know enough about you
Do I know enough about love

"You say it isn't always true, sometimes we have different doubts. I know what you're saying to me, but don't count this moment out"

REFLECTIONS OF A BAD DAY

What's the point of this tonight
Seems a day gone by and masked
Behind a crooked smile
And a darkened glass
What's the point of this tonight
You just can't make it go
Losing sleep in your daydreams
Won't change it all you know

Your mind feels crushed
Your smile it fades to grey
The sun points to darkness
Reflections of a bad day
The salts a bitter taste
The tears run dry and hey
It's all right going over
Reflections of a bad day

What's the point of this tonight
The silence in your words
You fall further down
Shadows of doubt are heard
Another moment falls tonight
A broken whisper away
Your lost sleep in your daydreams
Won't change your yesterday

Your mind feels crushed
Your smile fades to grey
The sun points down to darkness
Reflections of a bad day
The salts a bitter taste
The tears run dry and hey
It's all right going over
Reflections of a bad day

Just can't break out from these feelings
It's so easy for you to say
It's all right to go over
Reflections of a bad day

Not Going Down Like The Sun

Feel it going down slowly
Like the sun behind a lonely hill
Like my faults falling one by one
Nothing seems to give me something like you do

Feeling it like an ocean breeze
Drifting like a full moon in the dark
Reflecting like emotions on the run
Feels like it hits real hard

And I can't breathe
But I have to be the strong one
Cause where I want to be is here
Not going down
Not going down like the sun

My hearts tied I know it's tight
But the strings are not attached
Like a fire I once fought within me
I followed the right path, the right map

And I can't breathe
But I have to be the strong one
Cause where I want to be is here
Not going down like the sun

Cause where I want to be is here
Not going down
Not going down like the sun

Piece Of Mind

Your tenderness
Like your kiss
It does me real harm
Broken pieces
I'm sensitive
You left me a big scar

It seems to go on forever
Now I can't take it back
I should have said now or never
But I got a little off track

But now that I can see
This was all wrong
I was a hopeless case
That caught me undone
I hope that you find
A place where the sun still shines
I hope that you find
A real piece of mind

You talk cheap
With no belief
I can't sleep at night
I'm in the back seat
The road is steep
Just doesn't seem right

It seems to go on forever
I should have said it now
But now I just cannot take it back

But now that I can see
This was all wrong
I was a hopeless case
That caught me undone
I hope that you find
A place where the sun still shines
I hope that you find
A real piece of mind

"I'm walking crooked, this straight line is bending, and my shoe is wearing thin. Replace it; replace this sole, with more than modern sin"

FROST

I've been around the bend
Feels like I'm on the move again
It all feels pretend
Sitting in this great big room
You want to know why
My silence makes a lonely sound
You want to know why
You've seen it all falling down

I'm on the run again, getting bent again
I'm on the mend my friend

It's four in the morning
Everything right now is not enough
The dark feels like frost
And you're not here to give me love
The dark feels like frost
And you're not here to hold me up

I've been around the bend
Jumped every hoop and sat on a big fence
It seems so bloody bent
I wonder if it makes any kind of difference

You want to know why
I feel the knife pushing in my chest
You want to know why
If it means any kind of difference

I'm on the run again, falling down again
I'm on the mend my friend

It's four in the morning
Everything right now is not enough
The dark feels like frost
And you're not here to give me love
The dark feels like frost
And you're not here to hold me up
The dark feels like frost
And you're not here to stop the crush

POLITICS

We seek to find, we run to hide
They rise, they fall
Does it matter at all

Politics, politics

I ask the minister
What's this collapse
What's this brains trust
What's the take on the economy

Politics, politics

Attack on the treasury
Details of the conversation
All over their heads
Defend with aggression

Freedom for all
The political leader falls
Stunned by the furor
I don't know if it's easing

Politics, politics

We seek to find, we run to hide
They rise, they fall
Does it matter at all

It's pretty fair they say
Just words of puffery
Its do or dare they pay
Stuff the world and its needs

Don't you believe them
They're just lying to you
They'll get their way
Their way has very little to do with your way
They're just politicians, it's all about politics
It's pretty fair they say, politics

ALL I CAN HOPE FOR

Memories are falling
Then it rains down on me
Stains all my dreams
And all that I stood for
I shouldn't be ashamed
Of all that I've done
We all make mistakes
Some just hurt a little more

So you want me to be a better man
Then give me another chance
You want to see me turn and change
What I did wasn't my best

Now all that I hope for
Is some kind of wish
To answer my call
That's all I can hope for

What's it going to take
To fade this to darkness
To make these bad dreams
Fall in a tight net
What's it going to take
To make it all seem right
It never really happened
And it's not all in vain

So you want me to be a better man
Then give me another chance
You want to see me turn and change
What I did wasn't my best

Now all that I hope for
Is some kind of wish
To answer my call
That's all I can hope for
Something that can fix
Broken dreams and lost thoughts
That's all I can hope for

The Sun Has No Light

Come around and see
Be my desperate companion
Take the clothes from me
And fold them in the meadows

When nobody believes me
I'll say goodbye to the frost
And if you can't trust me
You might see the birds in the dusk

This sun has no light
This sun only gives shade
Like a lost minnow on the ocean
The sun gives nothing away
The sun has no light
The sun has no shade
Like a drying river
The suns falling away

I wrapped a warm moment
In a cold paper bag
And I took too long to notice
The strangers counted on my hand

And I strapped lost sleep
Triggered with my fingers
Before a shadow lost inside me
I moved like a flooded fever
Like a flooded fever

This sun has no light
This sun only gives shade
Like a lost minnow on the ocean
The sun gives nothing away
The sun has no light
The sun only gives shade
Like a drying river
The suns falling away
Like a drying flower
The suns falling away

RELEASES

~

Songs from Michael's lyrics are available on these artists' albums, EPs and singles and are available in the iTunes store worldwide:

Schism "Perpetual Devotion"

"Crystal Glass"

Vybornova Kristina "In Your Arms Again"

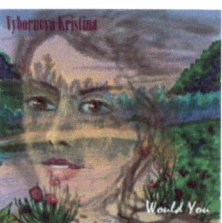

"Would You"

Harvey Welsh "Now Or Never"

"Second Skin"

Vybornova Kristina "Fall From Grace"

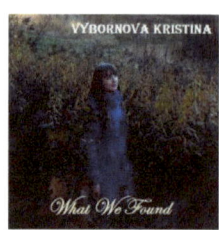

"What We Found"

Vybornova Kristina "My Breath"   Jeanne Fories "Piece Of Mind"

 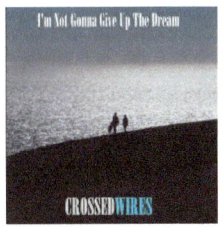

Arthur May "Enough About Love"   CrossedWires "I'm Not Gonna
                                   Give Up The Dream"

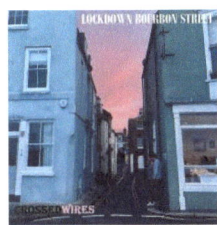 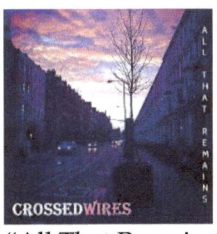

CrossedWires "Lockdown Bourbon Street"   "All That Remains"

Harvey Welsh "The Sun Has No Light"   "Frost"

Harvey Welsh "Yesterday's Sins"

ACKNOWLEDGEMENTS
~

Lyrics from the book are recorded by the following artists:

Harvey Welsh

A Life Filled With Love, Yesterday's Sins, Second Skin,
Bend And Change, Paint That Look, When You Know Who You Are,
Back Then, It's True, Catch Me, Now Or Never, Why, Lost Together,
In A Minute, Scream Louder, What's Going On, Ballad Of Surprise,
Tell Me, Together We Can Shine, Not Going Down Like The Sun,
Feeling Lonely, Frost, Politics, All I Can Hope For,
The Sun Has No Light

Richard Johnstone

Stone In My Shoes, Bleeding, Emerald Bay, Bridge To No-Where,
In The Rain, I'm Not Gonna Give Up The Dream,
Don't Be Too Afraid, Where The River Used To Go,
No Trouble At All, The Last Words, I'll Try Not To Say Too Much,
Preying For Love, I Don't Call This House My Home,
Stranger In My Dreams, Pretending You Know My Name, Crime City,
Our Own Eyes, Elaine, Blues In My Veins, Don't Go Losing Hope,
All That Remains, While The City Sleeps, Hurt Me Breaking The Rules

Vybornova Kristina

In Your Arms Again, Fall From Grace, Would You,
My Breath, What We Found

Schism

Harmony, Perpetual Devotion, Cold Silence, Desperation,
Crystal Glass, Bourbon Street, Don't Let It Go Tonight

Jeanne Fories

Piece Of Mind

Arthur May

Enough About Love

Trisha Roldan

Some Reason Now, Stranded Heart, Yesterday's News, Remember, Stir Crazy

Tamera Edwards

Reasons

Paul Lyons

Perpetual Devotion, A Life Filled With Love

Tom Girard

Every Moment I Get Closer, Broken And Busted, Where The River Used To Go

CrossedWires

Lockdown Bourbon Street, All That Remains, I'm Not Gonna Give Up The Dream

I would like to acknowledge and thank the following:

My dear children: Justin, Kristy, and Cassandra; My partner: Janelle Watson; Mum and Dad: Darryl and Moira Peade; Craig Peade, Blake Riley Langdon, Harvey Welsh, Richard Johnstone, Shannon Jackson, Stuart Johnson, Steve "Stuz" Zacka, Louise Little, Philippe Rizzo, Jeffrey Hopp, Kev Farley, Kevin Neil, Griffin Promotions, WK Digital, and Telstra. *You have helped, inspired, supported, and taught me valuable lessons over time.*

In loving memory of:

Ronald Hamilton *1912-1989* & Gwendoline Millicent Pead *1912-2013*
Edward Arthur *1901-1972* & Linda Phyllis Graham *1908-1978*

Greatly inspired by these music writers and artists:

Bernie Taupin, Paul Stanley, Rob Thomas, Steve Kilbey, Elton John, Neil Diamond, Ross Wilson, Joe Elliott, Paul Doucette, Def Leppard, Daniel Johns and Kiss.

Inner pages photography by:

Janelle Andrea Watson
i, *circa 2015*
18, *circa 2008*
50, *circa 2009*
86, *circa 2013*
94, *circa 2008*
106, *circa 2016*
Back page, *circa 2017*

Chris Kuhlmann
26, *circa 1996*
26, *circa 1996*

Justin Peade
62, *circa 2014*

Author
42, *circa 1996*
62, *circa 2010*
118, *circa 2017*

Sharon Woodward
74, *circa 2000*
127, *circa 2000*

Amy Galloway
133, *circa 2014*

Guest musicians on recordings:

Reginald Thornhill
Guitar, Perpetual Devotion, *(Paul Lyons recording)*

Morten Lonaas
Guitar, In Your Arms Again

Song releases cover art and photography by:

Richard Johnstone: Perpetual Devotion, Lockdown Bourbon Street, All That Remains, I'm Not Gonna Give Up The Dream.
Sharon Woodward: Crystal Glass. *Vybornova Kristina:* In Your Arms Again, Would You, Fall From Grace, What We Found, My Breath.
Jeanne Fories: Piece Of Mind. *Arthur May:* Enough About Love.
Michael J. Peade: Now Or Never, The Sun Has No Light.
Harvey Welsh: Second Skin, Yesterday's Sins.
Akka Ballenger Constantin: Frost.
All song cover designs by: *Michael J. Peade*
(Except, Perpetual Devotion, *Richard Johnstone,* Piece Of Mind, *Jeanne Fories*)

Michael lives on the Gold Coast, Queensland, Australia. He continues to write with many international producers, writers, musicians and performers.

www.songcastmusic.com/profiles/peadesongs
www.facebook.com/peadesongs
www.facebook.com/seedsofsongs

© Michael J. Peade 2020
© PEADESONGS

www.ingramcontent.com/pod-product-compliance
Lightning Source LLC
Chambersburg PA
CBHW041613220426
43670CB00001B/6